Athletic

Tillie Baldwin

LILLIAN RIGGS

INDEPENDENT

Lucille Mulhall

Charmayne James

GREATEST

MARY FIELDS

LEGENDARY

CALAMITY JANE

TALENTED

Johanna July

SALLY SKULL

RUGGED

Charley Parkhurst

Tad Lucas

ANNIE OAKLEY

GEORGIE CONNELL SICKING

COWBOY PETE

REBEL *in a* DRESS

BY

SYLVIA BRANZEI

ILLUSTRATED BY

MELISSA SWEET

RP|KIDS

PHILADELPHIA • LONDON

TO MY #1 COWGIRL, LUCY MANTHA,
may you always be filled with inspiration and joy.

AND TO MY FRIEND JAYDA WOOD,
who made me get on a horse and ride.

—S. B.

Printed in China

Books published by Running Press are available at special discounts for bulk purchases in the United States by corporations, institutions, and other organizations. For more information, please contact the Special Markets Department at the Perseus Books Group, 2300 Chestnut Street, Suite 200, Philadelphia, PA 19103, or call (800) 810-4145, ext. 5000, or e-mail special.markets@perseusbooks.com.

ISBN 978-0-7624-3695-8

Library of Congress Cataloging-in-Publication Number 2009923890

E-book ISBN 978-0-7624-4384-0

9 8 7 6 5 4 3 2 1
Digit on the right indicates the number of this printing.

Cover and interior design by Maria Lewis and Frances J. Soo Ping Chow
Typography: Helvetica, Just Me Down Here Again, Lady Rene, Mighty to Save, Pointy, Pea Bethany's Doodles, Sue Ellen Fransico, Trash Hand, and Trixie
Edited by T. L. Bonaddio and Lisa Cheng

Published by Running Press Kids
an imprint of Running Press Book Publishers
A Member of the Perseus Books Group
2300 Chestnut Street
Philadelphia, PA 19103-4371

Visit us on the web!
www.runningpress.com

CONTENTS

COWGIRL UP (v.):

To step up to the challenge,
to toughen up, to take charge of
a situation, to not give up

"A gal's gotta do what a gal's gotta do."

—Minnie Cody, pioneer, 1901

The women in this book have all ridden horses, but that is not the only thing they have in common. All of them share the cowgirl spirit, a strong will, and an independent heart. If you told one of these ladies she couldn't do it because she's a girl, she'd prove you wrong every time. They refused to take no for an answer. All of the women you will meet loved the thrill of the ride and the enchantment of adventure. These women are real-life examples of the cowgirl inside every one of you.

GEORGIE CONNELL SICKING

ACCOMPLISHED

COWBOY POET

I know what it is to ROPE a WILD Mustang... and I know what it is to Rock a baby. I think I've TRULY LIVED.

GeoRgie Connell Sicking
(b. 1921)

In January 1985, Georgie Connell Sicking found herself standing upon a stage before a crowd of hundreds. She and the other poets "were like a bunch of colts that had just been weaned, just hanging all together, nervous and scared." Georgie had been selected to represent Nevada in the first Cowboy Poetry Gathering in Elko, Nevada. It was her turn. She held up her paper and read:

Georgie in 2009, Florence, AZ.

"When I was a kid and doing
      my best to
Learn the ways of our land,
I thought mistakes were
      never made by
A real top hand...."

—Georgie Connell Sicking, from "To Be a Top Hand"

Georgie in 1987, Elko, NV.

The lady cowboy poet lost her place. Georgie had roped mustangs, broken horses, and killed rattlesnakes. She was an accomplished cowboy, a top hand. But now she shook with nerves. Georgie looked at the anxious crowd and started once again to read her poem "To Be a Top Hand." On that day, Georgie Connell Sicking added "ACCOMPLISHED cowboy poet" to her list of talents.

Georgie Connell Sicking Tidbit

An hour-long documentary film about Georgie's life called RIDIN' AND RHYMIN' was released in 2004.

Photo of Georgie taken at a carnival on her first date ⟶ with her future husband.

Georgie had known ranching all of her life. At the age of two, her parents had Georgie on horseback, teaching her to ride. By the age of five, she had her first horse, Buster.

Buster liked biscuits. Georgie would take a biscuit out to Buster and drop it on the ground. When he lowered his head to eat, the little girl scrambled up his neck and onto his back. Georgie rode her horse to school. In school, the girls learned "inside work," which wasn't much to Georgie's liking. Georgie knew what she wanted. She wanted to be a master cowboy, or top hand.

Georgie learned the cowboy skills. By the time she was seventeen, Georgie's parents had divorced. Her father remarried and left, leaving Georgie and her fifteen-year-old brother to fend for themselves. She tried to get cowhand work, but no one would hire a girl. Even though he was two years younger, her brother found work. So Georgie stayed behind and took care of the

Georgie in 1939 at age 18, during a steer riding in Victorville, CA.

She was always there before me, like a beacon in
    the distance.
A challenge that forever led me on.
I never really knew her, but the cowboys talked
    about her in a way that I was hoping that someday
    they'd mention me.

Lora was a cowboy in the ways that were before me.
By profession, not by gender she was known.
She didn't slow down for me, for she knew not that I'd
    Follow.
But she left a trail for me both wide and deep....

Now when she was riding way up yonder looking down
    beneath her,
Did she see the kid that followed on her trail?
Does she know I worked a little harder, and went a little
    further,
Because Lora left a legend that the cowboys tell?

—Georgie Connell Sicking, from "Lora and the Inspiration," 2004

on-site work. Alone she had to shoe the horses, doctor the animals, and rope and
tie the cattle.

When times were hard, Georgie recalled the stories she had heard about Lora
Duncan, a true lady cowboy. Georgie also wrote poetry about her experiences and
her inspirations.

Be Yourself

When I was young and foolish,
The women said to me,
"Take off those spurs and comb your hair,
If a lady you will be."

"Forget about those cowboy ways,
Come and sit awhile.
We will try to clue you in,
On women's ways and wiles."

"Take off that Levi jumper,
Put up those batwing chaps.
Put on a little makeup and,
We can get a date for you, 'perhaps.'"

"Forget about that roping,
That will make calluses on your hands.
And you know it takes soft fingers,
If you want to catch a man!"

"Do away with that Stetson hat,
For it will crush your curls.
And even a homely cowboy wouldn't,
Date a straight haired girl."

Now being young and foolish,
I went my merry way.
And I guess I never wore a dress,
Until my wedding day.

Now I tell my children,
No matter what you do.
Stand up straight and tall,
Be you, and only you.

For if the Lord had meant us, all to be alike,
And the same rules to keep,
He would have bonded us all together,
Just like a band of sheep.

—Georgie Connell Sicking, 1985

> "I know what it is to rope a wild mustang and have him hit the end of the rope, and I know what it is to rock a baby. I think I've truly lived."
>
> —Georgie Connell Sicking

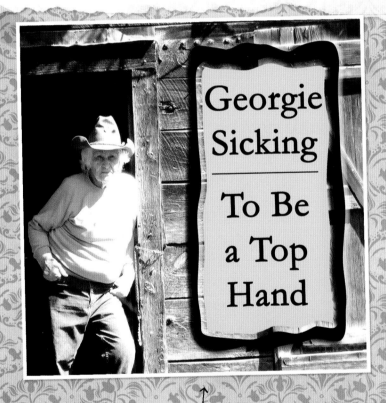

CD cover for Georgie Sicking's
TO BE A TOP HAND

In 1940, Georgie married Frank Sicking. Frank worked for the Green Cattle Company. Even though the company did not officially hire Georgie, she and Frank worked as a team. After two years of hard work, Georgie was given a cow for her efforts. The couple left the Green Cattle Company but returned several years later. This time Georgie was officially hired.

The cowboys in the outfit were not too happy. When Georgie was given a mount to ride, she went right to work to shoe him. The cowboys found all kinds of excuses to go into the barn and spy on Georgie. Georgie proved she could do the work of a cowboy, but some of the workers still didn't like it. When she said to her boss maybe she should leave, he told her "Listen, as far as I'm concerned you're the best hand I've got. . . . If these fellas don't want to work with you, they can go out the same way they came in." Georgie Connell Sicking had achieved her goal—to be a top hand.

> **Also in 1985**
> * Coca-Cola replaces its ninety-nine-year-old formula with a sweeter one designed for younger tastes.
> * Compact discs and CD players are introduced as new technology.

Forty years later the ACCOMPLISHED lady cowboy told of her experience through her poems. The poetry she had written for herself she now shared at cowboy poetry gatherings. And the attentive audience listened to the top hand.

AMAZING

ANNIE OAKLEY

AIM AT A HiGH MARK AND YOU WiLL Hit it

LiTTLE SURE SHOT

ANNIE OAKLEY
(1860–1926)

BUFFALO BILL'S WILD WEST·
CONGRESS, ROUGH RIDERS OF THE WORLD.

MISS ANNIE OAKLEY,
THE PEERLESS LADY WING-SHOT.

← Poster for Buffalo Bill's Wild West·Congress, Rough Riders of the World. Printed at bottom: Miss Annie Oakley, The Peerless Lady Wing-Shot.

← American sharpshooter Phoebe Ann Mosey, better known as Annie Oakley, 1899.

O n May 11, 1887, a slightly built woman greeted her audience by waving and blowing kisses. She was dressed modestly with a western flair. Like a good Victorian woman, her blouse was buttoned high and her thick stockings completely covered her legs. She had spent hours embroidering the designs on her skirt and her shirt. She skipped across the open-air stage, picked up a rifle, and started shooting at her target. She never missed. She was Annie Oakley, the most AMAZING sharpshooter who had ever lived.

The audience she performed to on that day in May was not the regular American crowd. Annie demonstrated her skills to honor the fiftieth anniversary

17

"For me, sitting still is harder than any kind of work."

—Annie Oakley

Annie Oakley   "Dave"

↰ Annie Oakley shoots an apple off the head of her dog, Dave.

of the queen of Great Britain's reign, the Golden Jubilee of Queen Victoria. The private show was for Queen Victoria herself. Queen Victoria watched as the modest Oakley split playing cards in half with a bullet and shot the ash off of a cigar held in the mouth of her assistant and husband, Frank Butler.

Annie Oakley and Queen Victoria were similar in several ways. Both women were very moderate in their dress and behavior. Yet both were successful in positions dominated by men. The queen was the ruler of a country. Annie Oakley was the master of a masculine skill, sharpshooting.

The two women were also significantly different. Queen Victoria was born into her position and Annie Oakley was born into poverty. Her name was not yet Annie Oakley; it was Phoebe Ann Mosey. She started shooting not for sport but for food. When she was barely big enough to lift her deceased father's rifle, Annie dragged it outside and hunted game to put food on the table for her mother and siblings. She was so skilled at shooting she started selling game to the local grocery store.

Annie Oakley Tidbit

Annie Oakley died on November 3, 1926. Her bereaved husband, Frank Butler, died eighteen days later.

Annie recalled one Christmas, "My stocking was so heavy it could not hang from the rail, but was laid on the table." Inside her Christmas stocking was a can of Black Powder, five pounds of shot, and two boxes of caps, "all a gift of the merchant who bought my game." She didn't go to school

Frank Butler

Circus poster, ca. 1896.

Also in 1881

* The Red Cross is founded by Clara Barton.

* The Barnum & Bailey Circus is created.

THE BARNUM & BAILEY GREATEST SHOW ON EARTH

THE WORLD-FAMOUS SILBONS

THE WORLD'S LARGEST, GRANDEST, BEST AMUSEMENT INST...

Miss Annie Oakley, dubbed "Little Sure Shot" by Chief Sitting Bull. ⟶

because she was busy hunting. By the time she was fifteen, she had earned enough money to pay off the amount owed on her mother's house.

To earn money, Annie also entered local shooting contests. She was so good her reputation spread throughout southern Ohio where she lived. In the spring of 1881, sharpshooter Frank E. Butler was

→ MISS ANNIE OAKLEY. ←
(LITTLE SURE SHOT)

J. WOOD, Photo.   208 Bowery, N. Y.

performing in southern Ohio. He boasted to the hotel owner that he could outshoot anyone around. The hotel owner knew otherwise. He agreed to Frank's challenge but didn't let on that the challenge would be against a young woman.

A large crowd showed up for the competition. Butler was shocked when the petite Annie stepped forward. She shot all twenty-five targets. Frank missed on his twenty-fifth shot and Annie won. Unlike most men in the late 1800s, Butler was not bitter at losing to a girl. He was awed. So much so, he started courting Annie. They were married a year later.

ANNIE GET YOUR GUN

* A Broadway musical very loosely based on Annie Oakley's life was a huge hit in 1946. Annie sings a song titled "You Can't Get a Man with a Gun." In the beginning of the show, she beats Frank Butler in a shooting competition. At the end of the show, she loses on purpose to the man that she loves. Then they get married.

* A movie version of ANNIE GET YOUR GUN was released in 1950. Except for having two sharpshooters named Annie Oakley and Frank Butler, it had nothing much to do with the real life of Annie Oakley.

Annie Oakley became known as "Little Sure Shot," a name given to her by Chief Sitting Bull when he adopted her into his tribe. For seventeen years, Annie and Frank performed with Buffalo Bill's Wild West Show. Annie thrilled the crowds wherever the show traveled. The crowds not only loved her, they also accepted her.

Little Sure Shot was an accurate name for Annie Oakley. She could shoot left- or right-handed. She hit her mark while riding bicycles or on the back of a running horse. She could hit a playing card from the thin edge and then shoot it six more times as it fell to the ground. If Frank tossed three eggs into the air, Annie would hit all three before they splattered upon the ground. Her mirror shot was a real crowd pleaser. Annie would turn her back on her target and place her rifle over her shoulder. Looking in a hand mirror, she would shoot and hit the target. Annie Oakley was an AMAZING markswoman.

"Aim at a high mark and you will hit it. No, not the first time, not the second, and maybe not the third. But keep on aiming and keep on shooting, for only practice will make you perfect. Finally, you'll hit the Bull's-Eye of Success."

—Annie Oakley

Annie demonstrates sighting a target with a mirror.

Poster from 1901, commemorates Annie's career with Buffalo Bill's Wild West and her extraordinary marksmanship feats.

ANNIE OAKLEY

A SPECIAL FEATURE
WITH
BUFFALO BILL'S WILD WEST

THE PEERLESS WING AND RIFLE SHOT

ASTOUNDING

Charley Parkhurst

IT'S THE WAY you ride THE trail THAT counts
--DALE EVANS

CHARLEY PARKHURST
(1812-1879)

On December 29, 1879, the retired delivery driver One-eyed Charley passed away in his small cabin near Watsonville, California. Through the last month of his illness, Charley had been tended to by his friend, Frank Woodward. Charley had requested that when he died he be buried in his everyday clothes, but that just didn't seem proper. As the body was prepared for burial, everyone who had known Charley over the last several decades was in for a big surprise. One-eyed Charley was actually Charlotte—a woman!

OLD CHARLIE.

Writer and illustrator J. Ross Browne holds tight as Charley Parkhurst drives the stage.

Woodward could hardly believe the truth about his old friend. Another of Charley's chums said he had shared a buffalo hide blanket with "Ol' Parkie" during a cold night and now he wondered a bit about his new partner, Curley Bill. Charley stunned everyone at death. But while alive she fooled no one about her

"From Mine to Mill," engraving from HARPER'S WEEKLY, September 14, 1878. Stagecoach and wagon drivers often navigated treacherous terrain and difficult weather conditions.

ability to handle horses pulling a coach loaded with goods and passengers. Charley was an **ASTOUNDING** stagecoach driver.

Driving a stagecoach took skill and guts. Women of the 1800s were expected to be dainty and well-mannered. Dainty and well-mannered Charley was not. She drank, chewed tobacco, smoked cigars, cussed, and gambled. She didn't choose the path of the gentlewoman dressed in hooped skirts. She chose to live in the man's world—in a line of work that took courage.

Her employee records said Parkhurst "was small (only about five feet and six inches), slim and wiry, with alert gray eyes." Charley did not speak much and never talked about her past. But that was not unusual in the West. Many people chose not to speak about their past. When she did speak, Parkhurst had "an oddly sharp,

"I found out that, if you want to do something badly enough, you're going to find a way."

—Sally Gibbs, cowgirl, 1887

high-pitched voice." In the mid-1800s, it would have never occurred to anyone that a woman might want to drive a stagecoach. Most people just thought it was a bit odd when Parkhurst would sleep with the horses rather than share a room with the rest of the drivers and that Charley chose to never grow a beard.

After the shocking discovery of Charley's gender, a search was conducted as to her true identity and details of her life were revealed. Charlotte Parkhurst was

Charley Parkhurst Tidbits

- Charley's tombstone simply reads PARKHURST.
- Parkhurst earned her nickname "One-eyed Charley" after a horse she was shoeing kicked her and took out her eye. She always wore a patch over her missing eye.

- In 1855, Charley Parkhurst registered to vote in the presidential election between Grant and Seymour. No records show if she cast a ballot, but if she did, Parkhurst voted almost fifty years before women had the right to vote in the United States.

Poster of Overland Mail
Route to California, 1866. →

Also in 1879

* Rolled toilet paper is produced in Great Britain.

* On New Year's Eve, three thousand people gather to see Edison's electric light display.

born in New Hampshire. She was orphaned at a young age. As a young woman, she dressed as a boy and got a job at a stable in Massachusetts. Maybe Charlotte realized it would be difficult for a woman to make it on her own, and she needed a profession. Maybe she liked horses, and Charlotte knew horsemanship was not an acceptable occupation for females in the 1800s.

Whatever her reason, Charlotte became Charles. Her employer, Ebenezer Balch, saw she was good with horses, so he trained her to drive coaches. Charley drove for Balch until 1851, when she went west to California.

Charley Parkhurst drove a stagecoach in California for twenty years, and she never had an accident. She was known as one of the fastest and safest drivers. Charley ruled a team of four to six horses. Riding in front, she was exposed to all weather. Her face was sun-baked. Her clothes became covered in dust and mud. Bad weather was just an inconvenience compared to many other perils faced on the roads of the Wild

West—attacks by Indians and robbers, encounters with wild animals, and head-on collisions with other coaches driving the one lane, curvy, mountain roads.

One time Charley crossed a narrow wooden bridge only to look back and see it collapse. Another time she fell from a moving coach but hung on to the reins. Charley was dragged along until she got the runaway horse team to stop.

She was held up by robbers only twice. The first time, she gave over the strongbox, a box with valuables. The next time, she was prepared. When the robber ordered the stagecoach to stop and hand over the strongbox, Charley pulled out a shotgun and blasted him in the chest. No one tried to hold up Charley Parkhurst ever again.

Charley Parkhurst was everything a stagecoach driver should be, rough and tough. And one thing a stagecoach driver wasn't expected to be, a female. ASTOUNDING!

"It's the way you ride the trail that counts."

—Dale Evans, cowgirl

↖ A reenactment of a stagecoach robbery illustrates some of the dangers awaiting drivers and passengers, ca. 1911.

Tillie Baldwin

You'll never do a whole lot unless you're brave enough to try. -DOLLY PARTON

Athletic

TILLIE BALDWIN
(1888–1958)

← Photographic postcard, "Fancy riding by Tillie Baldwin Champion Lady Buckaroo." 1912.

You don't think twice about slipping on a pair of pants. You, your mother, and your grandmother all wear pants. For riding a horse, a pair of jeans is the obvious choice. Yet in the early 1900s, things were very different; ladies wore long dresses. Pants were not an option. Even rodeo women competed in cumbersome long skirts as they roped steer and ran relay races.

Some of the cowgirls had taken to wearing split skirts, which were long dresses, cut up at the center and sewn back together to make long culottes. However, split skirts hindered movement, which made trick riding, relay racing, and bronc riding dangerous.

ROMAN RACE. RIDERS JOHNIE MULLENS, TILLIE BALDWIN & A.J. BRYSON. WINNIPEG STAMPEDE 1913.

Tillie leads the Roman race, Winnipeg Stampede, → Manitoba, Canada, August 1913.

"I don't like bloomers or bloomer women, but I think that sport and healthful exercise make women better, healthier and happier."

—Annie Oakley

Misses' and girls' gymnastic costume, 1900 →

Tillie in her athletic outfit, 1913

Athletic Bloomers

Bloomers were the first women's sporting outfits. In the late 1800s, women started wearing knee-length baggy trousers that fastened below the knee. Bloomers were to be worn for the limited athletic activities women were allowed to participate in, such as bicycle riding and gymnastics.

In 1912, Tillie Baldwin appeared in the Pendleton Roundup wearing bloomers! For the last two years, Tillie had competed in bronc and trick riding. She was good. Just the year before, she won her first bronc riding competition. But her new attire would give Baldwin an edge over the cowgirls in split skirts, and she liked to win.

Tillie Baldwin Tidbit

Tillie Baldwin quit rodeoing after she got married. For many years, she taught horse riding near her home in Connecticut.

Tillie designed an outfit similar to the gym suits and bicycling outfits worn by a handful of daring women at the turn of the century. The bloomers had elastic below the knees so Tillie could perform handstands for the trick riding competitions and her clothes would not get caught in the stirrups while riding broncos. Her choice of clothing allowed Tillie to use her excellent ATHLETIC talents to the fullest. And she did.

Tillie Baldwin was not your typical cowgirl. Unlike most of the rodeo cowgirls, Tillie Baldwin did not grow up on a ranch. She wasn't even born in North America. Tillie Baldwin was born as Mathilda Winger in Avendale, Norway. She emigrated from Norway to New York as a teenager. During an outing on

Map of Norway

Staten Island, Mathilda saw Hollywood cowgirls practicing trick and bronc riding. Even though she had never been on a horse, Mathilda knew what she wanted to do. She wanted to become a cowgirl.

As a girl in Norway, she was very athletic. She skied, skated, and canoed. As a young woman in the United States, she learned to use her athletic talents for trick riding.

Once she joined a Wild West Show, Mathilda Winger became Tillie Baldwin. She quickly became the star of the 101 Ranch Wild West show. But Tillie wanted competition. In 1911, she competed in her first rodeo. Baldwin won the bronc riding event.

In her new bloomer outfit, Tillie Baldwin won both the trick riding and the bronc riding competitions at the 1912 Pendleton Roundup. Tillie became one of

4048

TILLIE BALDWIN ON NO SIR,
STAMPEDE CALGARY 1913

Top: "Tillie Baldwin, Champion Lady Buckaroo," Pendleton, OR, 1912.

Bottom: Tillie Baldwin on "No Sir," Stampede Calgary, Canada, 1919.

the greatest cowgirl bronc riders of the time. Even so, Tillie expanded into other areas of competition. At the 1913 Winnipeg Stampede, she entered the standing Roman race, the first woman to ever do so.

For the standing Roman race, the rider planted one foot on the back of two different horses. The horse team with the rider standing atop stampeded around a half-mile track. Races ran everyday and the rider with the best time at the end of the Stampede was declared the winner.

The Winnipeg Tribune reported that Tillie "drove her twin mounts at a gait that would frighten many men . . . to death." After one race, Tillie collapsed. She was taken to the hospital. The doctors told her she needed to rest for several days. However, Tillie Baldwin was back in the arena the following day and newspapers reported it was her best day at the Stampede. At the end of the Stampede, Tillie Baldwin had beaten her male competitors to become the champion.

After her success at the standing Roman race, Tillie tried bulldogging. Again she was the first woman to try this very dangerous event. Bulldogging was invented by Bill Perkins, a famous black cowboy. The bulldogger rode on

Also in 1912

* Arizona and New Mexico become states.

* The RMS TITANIC sinks.

FANCY ROPING BY TILLIE BALDWIN & HORACE DAY. "STAMPEDE" WINNIPEG 1913

↰ Fancy roping by Tillie Baldwin and Horace Day, Winnipeg Stampede, August 1913.

horseback into the arena with a steer running about. The bulldogger would leap from the horse onto the back of the steer, grab it by its horns, and wrestle it to the ground. Not many cowgirls followed Tillie's example. It would be more than a decade before the next female bulldogger, Fox Hastings, would make a name for herself at this rugged rodeo sport.

The ATHLETIC Tillie Baldwin was a self-made cowgirl. Her competitive and adventurous spirit motivated Tillie to try things no other cowgirl of her era would—bloomers and bulldogging.

FEARLESS

Tad Lucas

I WOULDN'T HAVE RIDDEN IF I FELT AFRAID. I WOULD HAVE QUIT RIGHT THEN.

TAD LUCAS
(1902–1990)

When the rodeo organizers of Pueblo, Colorado, invited "Rodeo's First Lady" to perform, Tad Lucas had to think for a moment. Could she trick ride again? It was less than a year since her accident.

At the Chicago's World Fair in 1933, while competing in trick riding, Tad chose to go under the horse's belly. This trick wasn't that hard for her and she had been doing it for eight years. But this time was different. Just as she got underneath her horse's belly, Tad dropped too low and the horse's hoof caught her. She was pulled down under the running hooves, and she tumbled along. The bones in her left arm shattered, and it took several operations to repair her arm. The doctors told the **FEARLESS** Tad Lucas she would never ride again.

Tad riding Angel, Springfield, MO, ca. 1945.

39

Tad Lucas Tidbits

◆ Tad retired from rodeo performing in 1958 at the age of fifty-six. She had the longest running career of any rodeo cowgirl.

◆ In 1935, Tad Lucas made $12,000 from performing contracts and winnings. In 1935, teachers earned $1,227, and doctors earned $3,382.

Postcard of Tad Lucas on Hell Cat, 1943.

Riding is all that Tad Lucas knew. Tad could never remember a time in her life when she did not ride. She was born in 1902, the youngest of twenty-four children. Her family was the first to settle in Cody, Nebraska. Her name was Barbara Inez Barnes, but her father nicknamed her Tadpole. By the age of seven, Tad was helping her brothers break colts.

On Saturday nights in Cody, Nebraska, there would be bronc busting and steer riding on Main Street. Tad remembered when she was around twelve, "They'd brought this bronc in. Now, my brother, he thought I could do anything. He said, 'Tad'll ride him.' I climbed on him, and of course he bucked me off." But that didn't stop the fearless girl; she kept climbing on broncos and steers trying to ride. At the age of fourteen, Tad was in her first steer-riding contest at the fair in Gordon, Nebraska. She won and later stated, "Well, that ruined me, right there."

Even though Tad was not born into a rodeo family, rodeo became her entire life. At first she rode broncos and steers. Later she added relay racing and trick riding.

Tad started trick riding when she was twenty-two. Tad loved to do daring tricks on her horse. She invented the "suicide drag," where the rider would hook her knees onto the back of the horse, then bend backward and hang upside down behind a galloping horse.

In 1925, Tad won the trick riding championship at Cheyenne, Wyoming, and continued to win for six years straight. For eight years in a row, she was the trick riding champion at Madison Square Garden. She also captured trophies and cups in bronc riding and relay racing.

Tad married steer wrestler and fellow bronc rider, Buck Lucas. They honeymooned on a ship bound for England with the Tex Austin's Wild West Show. Together Tad and Buck Lucas traveled the rodeo circuit. When their daughter Mitzi was born, Tad Lucas would put the infant in her cowboy hat and ride her around the arena during the grand entry parade. Mitzi had her own pony by the age of two. Mitzi Lucas would be like her mother. She would never remember a time when she did not ride.

Tad Lucas in a studio portrait, ca. 1935.

"This is the life I've been looking for, the continual challenge! I love it."

—Vera McGinnis, horse relay racer

Tad Lucas Award

In 1990, after the death of her mother, Mitzi Lucas Riley created the Tad Lucas Award. Riley stated, "I just wanted to honor women who had contributed to the rodeo, who had kept it alive."

Also in 1933

* More than 25,000 Dy-Dee-Dolls sell. The doll sucks water from a bottle, then wets its diaper.

* DayGlo colors are invented.

Before her accident in 1933, Tad Lucas was the champion all-around cowgirl at Madison Square Garden for five years running. Rodeo was what made her blood run. And she wasn't about to stop just because of a severely broken arm. Tad agreed to perform in the rodeo at Pueblo, Colorado. Although her arm was in a heavy cast, Tad told the organizers that she knew several tricks she could do with one hand, like the suicide drag and the shoulder stand, and that her six-year-old daughter Mitzi could do tricks as well. Tad Lucas performed at the rodeo along with her daughter, where she "dressed her up in little shorts and a little fancy blouse, and the crowd just loved her."

Tad Lucas and her daughter Mitzi would go on to perform trick riding together for twenty years. Tad would also continue to compete in bronc riding. And she would continue to win. Tad Lucas, the FEARLESS cowgirl, was the most successful woman in rodeo history.

Petticoats
Are no bar to progress
in either writing
or ranching

Lucille Mulhall

FIRST

Lariats.

No. 93450 **Rawhide** iats, 4 plaits, best qual of oil tanned, rawhi center, all hand plai and whole strands fr end to end withont sp ing; rawhide hond length 40 ft., weight, lbs. each, $7.20. Leng 43 ft., weight 2½ lbs., ea $7.74. Length, 45 weight, 3 lbs., each, $8. Any length lariats ma to order.

No. 93451 **Cotton laria** extra quality braided ce ton rope. ½ inch diameter, honda of same, secure fastened; length 35 ft., each....................$1. Length 50 ft., each.....................2.

No. 93452 **Linen Lariats**, extra quality braid linen rope, ¾ inch in diameter, with rawhide hond have been boiled in oil, which keeps them soft a pliable, and renders them water proof; will not ki or snarl, and will hold anything that runs on ho Ends are patent grip fastened.
Length forty feet, each.....................$2.
Length fifty feet. each.....................2.
No. 93452½ **Hondas for Lariats**, firmly pressed ra hide. Each.....................$0.

LUCILLE MULHALL
(1885-1940)

The crowd at the 1904 Fort Worth, Texas, cattle convention anxiously waited. When the first steer ran into the arena, Lucille Mulhall was already mounted on her horse, ready. She twirled her lariat in a large circle above her head, threw it right on target, and caught the steer by the horns. Lucille jumped down from her horse, grabbed the rope attached to her side, and quickly hogtied the steer. She signaled she was done by throwing her arms up in the air.

Lucille Mulhall after completing a steer roping.

Her time was one minute and forty-five seconds. The next steer was better, one minute and eleven seconds. And the last one she cinched in forty seconds!

The eighteen-year-old "slight girl, who weighs barely more than one hundred pounds, had caught and tied her three steers in the splendid time of three minutes and thirty-six seconds." Lucille Mulhall beat out all of her cowboy competition in Fort Worth, Texas. She set a new time record. Lucille Mulhall, Queen of the Range, took home the championship gold medal and another FIRST place in steer roping.

When she was only sixteen, Lucille beat all of the cowboys to win her first steer roping competition. After her record-setting win in Fort Worth, she went on to Denison, Texas. An old cowboy who saw her there said, "First woman I'd ever seen that wasn't on a side saddle. . . . And she was a fine steer tier. She could

"Little Miss Mulhall, who weighs only ninety pounds, can break a bronco, lasso and brand a steer, and shoot a coyote at 500 yards. She can also play Chopin, quote Browning, construe Virgil, and make mayonnaise dressing. She is a little ashamed of these latter accomplishments . . ."

—*New York World* (1900), about Lucille Mulhall

Cowgirls vs. the Ladies

Until they went to the Wild West, women who rode horses used side-saddles. Seeing a woman ride astride was quite scandalous.

At the turn of the century, women wore long dresses and skirts. As this was not convenient for riding horses, cowgirls slit their long skirts up the middle and sewed them together to make "divided skirts." In 1895, a ranch woman who rode into Miles City, Montana wearing a divided skirt reported, "A warning was given to me to abstain from riding on the streets of Miles City lest I might be arrested!"

rope those steers, drag 'em down, and tie 'em just like a man." She competed against thirty cowboys and won.

Lucille learned to ride and rope from the cowboys and ranch hands on her father's 80,000-acre ranch in Oklahoma. Part of the year, she was sent away to boarding school where she learned poetry and manners. Lady stuff wasn't much to Lucille's liking. She wanted to be on the ranch. Her father, Zack Mulhall, claimed that when his daughter was thirteen, she asked him for her own herd of cattle. He told her she could keep any of his cattle that she could capture and brand in one day. By the end of that one day, three hundred cows were wearing Lucille's brand.

Lucille Mulhall Tidbits

- Mulhall is a town in Oklahoma named after Lucille's father. In the old bank is Lucille's Restaurant.
- When she was fifty-five years old, Lucille Mulhall died less than a mile away from the Mulhall Ranch in a car accident.

Performing before crowds at the competitions was no problem for Lucille. She had performed in her father's Wild West shows since she was thirteen. At the age of fourteen, she rode and roped before the future president, Theodore Roosevelt. He was so impressed he called her the "world's most expert horsewoman."

Roosevelt visited the Mulhall Ranch and befriended the family. During one visit, legend has it that Roosevelt admired a wolf he saw while riding with the horsewoman. Lucille roped the wolf for the future president. When he became president, the Mulhall family rode in his inaugural parade.

In 1905, the *New York Times* reported that Lucille Mulhall would "appear in Madison Square Garden simply to show what a Western girl can do who has been trained among horses all her life." Compared to competing in the arenas against men, this performance was simple for Mulhall. However, it was new to many of the Easterners.

Lucille wowed the audiences with her western skills. However, the newspapers didn't quite know how to label the new sensation. Reporters referred to her as the "Female Conqueror of Beef and Horn," "Ranch Queen," and "Cowboy Girl." Finally "cowgirl" appeared. The word had been used

Also in 1905

* Canned baked beans are introduced in England.

* A play about a saloon girl falling in love with a bandit, called THE GIRL OF THE GOLDEN WEST, opens in Pittsburgh.

almost a decade earlier, but it had never caught on. "Cowgirl" was to become the term associated with females that rode horses. But in 1905, the word was perfect for describing "Zack Mulhall's pretty daughter, who can ride a bronco and lasso a steer with any cowboy in the Territory." Lucille Mulhall earned the title of "America's FIRST cowgirl."

← Lucille Mulhall in a photo by Murillo Studio, St. Louis, MO, ca. 1905.

It was something that I excelled in and I put a lot of time in.

Charmayne James

BARRELS ↑

GREATEST

CHARMAYNE JAMES
(b. 1970)

Eleven-year-old Charmayne James climbed on the back of the horse with an attitude. Charmayne knew how to ride. She had been on the back of a horse since she was three. For the last two years, she had competed in barrel races with a powerful horse that used to belong to her older sister. Now it was time for a horse of her own.

This one looked like a good horse, but he had a bad reputation. The horse had landed his first owner in the hospital. Another owner sold him because he didn't like the look in the horse's eyes. The horse had ended up in Clayton, New Mexico, where he would work herding cattle from the pen into trucks. Charmayne's father, Charlie, had spotted Scamper while working at the feedlot, and he had thought of his daughter.

↖ Charmayne James waves to the crowd at the Wrangler National Finals Rodeo in Las Vegas as she officially retires Scamper from the arena.

Charlie warned his daughter to take it easy on the first ride. Charmayne only heeded her father's warnings for a moment. She states, "As soon as I got behind the barn and out of sight, I kicked him right into a lope. Scamper bucked a little and I laughed. When I laughed, he just kind of looked back at me like 'Oh, it's just you' and went right on without any trouble."

Her father recalls, "She rode the buck out of him, and I guess he just knew she wasn't scared of him." She took the $1,100 horse home.

Charmayne trained Scamper how to barrel race. Two weeks later, they entered a local competition and won. "I could read him. I always knew exactly what he was going to do, and I wasn't afraid of him. We just had a bond. He was a crazy horse and I was half crazy in love with horses. We fit," explains Charmayne. Together, Charmayne and Scamper would go on to win ten World

Charmayne James Tidbits

- Charmayne now trains other barrel racers to become better riders through clinics, books, and videos.
- Scamper was named to SPORTS ILLUSTRATED 25 Greatest Sports Animals list.
- Charmayne cloned Scamper, and on August 8, 2006, Clayton was born.

Charmayne James

Charmayne's Individual Records

#1 leading money earner in barrel racing until December 2010

First cowgirl to earn $1,000,000 (1990)

#1 winner of single-event professional rodeo championships (11)

#1 in consecutive professional championships (10)

First WPRA member to earn #1 back number (1987)

First WPRA member listed in *The Guinness Book of World Records* (1987 and 1992)

#1 WPRA record for the most NFR Qualifications (19 consecutive)

#1 holder of World Championships compared to all women in professional sports

Championships in barrel racing. Charmayne James would become the first million-dollar cowgirl and the GREATEST barrel racer in rodeo history.

Barrel racing is the only all women's event on the rodeo tour. A rider and her horse race around three barrels in a cloverleaf pattern and then run back to the finish line. The fastest time wins. A five-second penalty is added for any barrel knocked over. Great runs are between thirteen and fifteen seconds. Riders earn money for how they do in each rodeo. At the close of the rodeo season, the rider with the most money takes home the title of World Champion.

In 1984, Charmayne was fourteen. It was her first year running barrels in the rodeo circuit. She and her mom traveled to rodeos covering about one hundred

Charmayne riding Scamper at the 1990 Wrangler National
Finals Rodeo in Las Vegas.

YEE-HAW!

thousand miles throughout Canada and the United States. Scamper was getting used to the running on the rodeo ground, but he seemed to fall often.

Also in 1984
* Apple's Macintosh computer is introduced.
* The game Trivial Pursuit goes on sale.

In Beaumont, Texas, Scamper fell coming into the second barrel. Charmayne slipped over the front of the saddle and onto his neck. She hung on for dear life as Scamper left the second and headed for the third barrel. "It was extremely embarrassing! I got him pulled up, but I'm sure Scamper was thinking, 'What the heck are you doing up there?'" describes Charmayne. At the age of fourteen, Charmayne James won her first title as World Champion Barrel Racer.

Charmayne's most remarkable run was in 1985. As Scamper entered the arena he scraped the bridle against the fence, causing the bridle to break. The bridle is what the rider uses to maneuver and stop the horse. James was like a race car driver without a steering wheel or brakes. The straps dangled between

"You must have a positive attitude, and you have to tell yourself you can do it."
—Shelby Janssen, barrel racing student of Charmayne James

Scamper's legs as he headed toward the first barrel. At the third barrel, Scamper spit out his bit. Scamper and Charmayne roared to the finish and had the fastest time of the round.

From 1984 to 1993, James took the World Champion Barrel Racer title. After ten years of racing and winning in the rodeo circuit, Scamper was too old to race. James retired him. As Scamper grazed in the pasture, Charmayne continued to train. The common belief in the rodeo community was it was more the horse than the rider. People did not think Charmayne could earn the championship again since she no longer raced with Scamper. But after trying different horses, she finally settled on Cruiser. Riding Cruiser, Charmayne, at the age of thirty-two, won the 2002 World Championship. It took eight years. When she retired from racing, her career earnings totaled more than $1.9 million, the most ever won by a barrel racer. That record was later beaten in December 2010 by Sherry Cervi, who became the first $2 million barrel racer.

Charmayne James credits much of her success to her horses. "No horse can compare to Scamper. He was just made to do it. He had the desire, the ability, the toughness to stay at the top."

The same thing could be said of Charmayne James, the GREATEST barrel racer of all times. She was just made to do it. She had the desire, the ability, and the toughness to stay at the top.

> "It was something that I excelled in and I put a lot of time in."
>
> —Charmayne James

In the remarkable 1985 incident, Scamper's bridle dangles ⟶ as he rounds the second barrel.

LILLIAN RIGGS

independent

When

I'M in a SADDLE
I feel I'm LIVING
again.

LILLIAN RIGGS
(1888-1977)

Lillian Riggs was in the cattle and guest ranch business. Lillian was still ranching at the age of seventy. She was also blind and severely hearing impaired. In 1942, at the age of fifty-four, Lillian lost her sight. Yet she kept on. Her husband died eight years later, but that didn't stop Lillian either. "Everybody thinks I'm crazy to carry on, but if I quit, how am I going to keep busy?" she asked. Lillian Riggs was one **INDEPENDENT** cowgirl.

Lillian lost most of her hearing by the age of thirty, yet she knew the sounds of the area deep in her being. Over the years, she had looked over the rugged, rocky land, so the sights were etched into her mind's eye. Lillian said she could see the ranch each day from her memories.

Lillian lived on the Faraway Ranch in Arizona since she was five months old.

Lillian Riggs, ca. 1918 ⟶

FARAWAY RANCH

← Faraway Ranch plans

Faraway Ranch, Erickson-Riggs
Ranch House, Cochise, AZ. ——→

In 1888, her parents homesteaded the ranch, which was forty miles from the

closest town. Lillian, her sister, and her brother worked the ranch as children.

They learned to rope, brand, doctor, and herd cattle. As adults they took over

the 7,000-acre homestead. After her brother and sister left, Lillian became the

boss lady of the Faraway.

Lillian Riggs often got down on her knees and touched the ground. If the

grass felt fresh and long, she knew it would be good pasture for the cattle.

With her hands, she could identify each of her cows. Lillian would feel the body

and check the teeth. From this information, she would determine which cattle to

sell or keep. If a cow became ill, Lillian listened to the breathing while a ranch hand described the cow's symptoms so Lillian could explain how to properly treat the animal.

Back at the main house, she sat at the head of the table as she hosted dinner for the visitors at her guest ranch. When her sister first suggested opening a dude ranch in 1918, Lillian was opposed. She thought people would look down on them because of their rugged lifestyle. However, the opposite was true. Visitors came to hike the rock formations and observe ranching firsthand. Years later Lillian said, "Our guest ranch has kept me in touch with the outside world, and many hundreds of interesting people I have met made up in part for the city environment I have missed."

A guest helps rope a calf. Faraway Ranch was both a guest ranch➞ and a working ranch with up to 500 cattle.

"Lillian Riggs was a timeless person. She was fearless, independent, and stubborn. And what an asset that trait can be to someone with her handicaps. She may have looked small and frail but she was steel."

—Sally Klump, friend of Lillian Riggs

Lillian Riggs Tidbits

- After operating for fifty-three years, the guest ranch closed in 1970. Lillian was eighty-two. However, she kept ranching for several more years.

- Lillian and her husband, Ed Riggs, promoted the idea of making much of the ranch land into a national park. Through their efforts the Chiricahua National Monument was established.

Horses were an important part of ranch life. Lillian learned to ride as a child, and she wasn't about to stop just because she couldn't see. Often she rode holding the reins in one hand and with her other hand she held a guide rope attached to another rider.

But sometimes she let go of the guide rope and galloped over the land she knew so well. "My big gray 'seeing-eye' horse, Britches, knows I cannot see. He knows it, and he takes advantage of it. But he is a good horse. He stops when the going is dangerous. He never gets excited. He carries me as if I were china," praised Riggs. Lillian enjoyed riding with Britches in cattle round-ups until her early eighties.

Lillian Riggs was self-sufficient in many ways, but she had to depend upon others to help run her business. She hired ranch hands, a cook, and a manager for the guest ranch. At the bank, Lillian instructed the teller how to fold the dollars so that she could identify the worth of each bill. When doing ranch business with someone for the first time, Lillian would give the person too much money. If the extra money was returned, Lillian knew she could trust that person.

Soon after Lillian lost her sight, a visitor to the guest ranch offered her a large, comfortable car. Lillian Riggs wrote in response to the offer. "Had you seen me pounding along in a Chevrolet pick-up over rough roads or none at all, starting at four a.m. yesterday and finishing around seven in the evening you would not be so much concerned about my comfort. But it was very nice of you to think of it and mention it to me. Incidentally, after a twenty-mile truck ride each way, I did about twenty miles on horse back, behind a bunch of cattle that we were moving from one range to another." Not much got in the way of Lillian Riggs's **INDEPENDENT** ways.

Also in 1942

* Walt Disney releases the movie BAMBI.

* The first jet airplane is tested.

← Lillian Riggs, on left, 1959

LEGENDARY

CALAMITY JANE

AS **A** **CHILD** I ALWAYS had a fondness for adventure

outdoor exercis

Wild Bill Hickok

WILD BILL HICKOK

CALAMITY JANE
(1852–1903)

At the mention of cowgirls, people often think of Calamity Jane. She is a **LEGENDARY** cowgirl. She was bigger than life, and she made certain of that by spreading tall tales of her adventures in the West. In her autobiography, Calamity said, "As a scout, I had a great many dangerous missions to perform, and while I was in many close places, always succeeded in getting away safely, for by this time I was considered the most reckless and daring rider and one of the best shots in the western country."

Calamity Jane seated with rifle as General Crook's scout, ca. 1895.

Calamity claimed she saved the life of Captain Egan, was the wife of Wild Bill Hickok, rode the Pony Express, and rescued a stagecoach after the driver had been killed. All of her adventures were based on real people or actual events. Calamity just embellished them a bit by making herself the heroine of the story, when in most cases she probably wasn't even present.

Although most of her adventures were completely fictional or at least greatly exaggerated, Americans from the 1800s until today have eaten it up. The character of Calamity Jane has appeared on-screen dozens of times and in numerous books. Calamity Jane would be very pleased to know she is still remembered as a legendary symbol for the Old West cowgirl.

Take away the make-believe parts and the tall tales, and you still have the life of a rugged and resourceful woman, Martha "Calamity" Jane Cannary. After both of her parents died, Martha Jane Cannary was on her own at the age of fifteen. As a teenager, she worked in Wyoming at a boarding house. One night she dressed as a soldier and appeared at a party. Women at this time could be fined for wearing men's clothes. Calamity Jane was lucky to only be kicked out for what she was wearing.

Also in 1898

* The first shots of the Spanish-American War are fired.

* The book WAR OF THE WORLDS by H. G. Wells is released.

After this event, Calamity Jane often defied the law by wearing men's clothes. In 1872, a wagon train captain in the Black Hills of South Dakota saw a twenty-year-old Calamity Jane driving a mule train wearing a buckskin suit. As an adult, Calamity had herself photographed wearing men's clothing and holding a rifle. Calamity Jane liked to shock people

← Jane on horseback, ca. 1901.

with her manner of dress. However, she was never arrested for it.

No one knows how she earned her nickname "Calamity Jane." Calamity claimed it was during the Nursey Pursey Indian outbreak when she galloped across the battlefield to rescue the wounded Captain Egan. Captain Egan, on recovering, laughingly said, "I name you 'Calamity Jane,' the heroine of the

"As a child I always had a fondness for adventure and outdoor exercise..."

—Calamity Jane

The Character of Calamity Jane

In 1877, the booklet THE BLACK HILLS AND AMERICAN WONDERLAND was written by Henry Maguire. In it Maguire described the colorful, real-life Calamity Jane.

The dime-novel writer, Edward Wheeler, read THE BLACK HILLS AND AMERICAN WONDERLAND. He must have liked the part about Calamity Jane as he wrote a larger than life Calamity Jane character into his western novels. Wheeler never even met the real Calamity Jane. And he never shared any of his earnings with Calamity Jane.

Plains." She also said "Calamity" referred to the trouble she always seemed to get herself into, which seems a more likely source for her nickname. For most of her life everyone called her Calamity Jane. Very few people even knew her real name.

Calamity Jane was not like the prim and proper women of the times. Keeping a house and caring for a family was not what she aspired to do with her life. She was a

Calamity Jane Tidbit

Calamity Jane requested that she be buried next to the "only man I ever loved," Wild Bill Hickok. Her friends honored her request.

Cowgirl Calamity Jane at Wild Bill Hickock's grave in Deadwood, SD. She was buried next to him in 1903.

Jane poses with her rifle, ca. 1895.

"Calamity Jane!!The Famous Woman Scout of the
Wild West!! The Terror of the Evildoers in the
Black Hills!! The Comrade of Buffalo Bill and
Wild Bill!! See this Famous Woman and Hear Her
Graphic Descriptions of Her Daring Exploits!"

—Advertisement from the Palace Museum, 1898

bullwhacker, a person who drove supply wagons. She tried prospecting for gold. She drank with the men in saloons. She gambled. And she entertained everyone with her storytelling skills.

The rowdy and wild Calamity Jane also had another side; she was kind and caring. When a smallpox epidemic broke out in Deadwood, South Dakota, the local women refused to treat the sick because they were afraid of contracting the disease. Calamity Jane cared for the ill day and night over many weeks. It was also said Calamity Jane would listen to people's troubles and offer comfort.

Calamity Jane lived all over the northwest. The newspapers of the day reported on her movements claiming, "Calamity Jane has arrived," and "Calamity Jane at Green River." As Calamity roamed the west, legends spread about her. She became a heroic character in western dime novels, which were very popular during this time. Calamity Jane took advantage of her superhero status by selling pictures of herself and appearing at dime museums and Wild West shows.

The ever-resourceful Calamity Jane released a short autobiography in 1896. She played up the heroic deeds so that she seemed more like the character portrayed in the popular books of fiction written about her. In her autobiography, Calamity made sure she was larger than life. She made sure she was LEGENDARY. But even without her tall tales, Calamity Jane would still be a renowned cowgirl.

SALLY SKULL

RUGGED

YOU'll LEARN NOTHIN' IF ONLY GOOD THINGS HAPPEN TO YOU. Mary C. Clayton, cowgirl

In 1823, when Sarah Jane "Sally" Newman was six years old, her family settled in northern Texas. The Native Americans of the area were not too pleased with people invading their land, and they wanted them out. The Native Americans stole the Newmans' horses, but the family didn't leave. Then the Comanche tried to enter through the front door. When Sally's mother, Rachel, saw toes under the front door, she grabbed an ax and scared the intruders away before they even came across the threshold.

↖ Palo Duro Canyon near Amarillo, TX.

Another time, they tried to come down the chimney. Rachel smoked them out with a flaming feather pillow. Sally learned if she wanted to survive in the West, she would have to be RUGGED.

> **"You better be good or Sally Skull is going to get you."**
>
> —Frontier mother's threat to her children

In just a few years, Sally could hold her own. One day, a male friend of the family was visiting when they spied two native warriors sneaking toward the house. Only Sally, her mother, her sister, and the visitor were home. The man

← John Rip Ford in his Confederate States Army uniform.

pretended his gun was broken, then said, "I wish I was two men, then I would fight those Indians." Sally answered back, "If you were one man, you would fight them. Give me that gun." Sally had learned the rugged lesson well. Some may say that she learned it too well.

In 1852, when Sally was thirty-five, she went to the Lone Star Fair in Corpus Christi, Texas. At the close of the fair, a pistol shot rang out. As people turned, they saw a man falling to the ground. Sally stood nearby holding a smoking gun.

The Texas politician and newspaper publisher, John Rip Ford, witnessed the event. He wrote, "She was a noted character named Sally Scull. She was famed as a rough fighter and prudent men did not willingly provoke her. It was understood that she was justifiable in what she did on this occasion, having acted in self defense."

Sally Skull Tidbits

- There are no photographs or drawings of Sally Skull.
- Some stories say that Sally killed her third husband and maybe even her second husband. Both just kind of disappeared.

Sally Skull was known for being deadly accurate when shooting with her left or right hand. And she wore two pistols on her hips at all times. Like in cowboy movies, Sally could draw, twirl her pistol, and shoot dead on. She was quick to shoot if provoked. And it didn't take a whole lot to upset her. When Sally found out about a cowboy saying bad things about her, she waited until the next time they met. Sally drew her gun on the cowboy. "Been talking about me, huh? Well, dance . . ." And the cowboy did a quick two-step as Sally shot at the ground around his feet.

Sally had developed a reputation as a woman not to be crossed. Dressed in rawhide bloomers and riding her horse astride, Sally journeyed across the border into Mexico to trade for horses. The route was dangerous and lawless. Sally was well armed. Large amounts of gold hung from her saddle horn. She traveled with only a couple of *vaqueros*, or Mexican cowboys. The small group rode into Mexico often, but no one ever troubled her.

After making a good trade for wild horses, Sally would kick up her heels in the small towns of Mexico. She loved to dance. It is said that she and her band of vaqueros raced through town on their horses, shooting and hooting all the way.

Talk of Sally Skull's skills, temper, and antics spread throughout Texas. A European tourist overheard a conversation in a hotel lobby. Intrigued, he asked for more detail and was told "of a North American amazon, a perfect female

Mexican horse race shows the VAQUEROS (cowboys) in colorful outfits, ca. 1900.

desperado. . . . She can handle a revolver and bowie-knife like the most reckless and skillful man, she appears at dances (*fandangos*) thus armed, and has even shot several men at merry makings."

Also in 1852
* Kerosene is made.
* UNCLE TOM'S CABIN by Harriet Beecher Stowe is published.

The rough and tough Sally married five different times in her life. From her first husband, Jesse Robinson, she learned about horses. He trained racehorses. She also had two children. Both children went to boarding school. Sally wanted her daughter to become a refined woman rather than follow in her mother's footsteps.

From her second husband, Sally Skull got her name. His name was George Scull. But Sally changed the spelling to Skull because she liked it better.

With her third husband, John Doyle, Sally took up ranching in 1852. It suited her fine for a couple of years. But land and livestock were not the life for Sally Skull.

Although accounts vary, it is believed that Sally married her fourth husband, Isaiah Wadkins, in 1855. They divorced three years later.

When Sally was in her forties, she married her last husband, Christoph Hordsdorff. In the late 1860s, Sally rode out of town with her husband. He came back, but she never did. Most people thought he shot her for her gold. But it was never proven. Sally Skull, the RUGGED horse trader, just disappeared.

No Shoes

TALENTED

Johanna July

I WAS YOUNG AND I WAS HAVIN' A GOOD TIME

Johanna July removed her bead necklaces, long gold earrings, and colorful dress. Her hair remained in a long black braid. She put on her bathing clothes. The teenage girl led the mustang into the waters of the Rio Grande. The water got deeper, and the wild horse started to swim. The swimming tired the horse and made it calmer. Johanna carefully swam up to the side of the horse, grabbed the mane, and eased up onto his back. She later recalled, "He couldn't pitch and when I did lead 'im out of dat deep water he didn't want to pitch." The mustang allowed a human to ride on his back for the first time. Johanna July was **TALENTED** at breaking horses.

Galloping →
wild horse

"I was young and I was havin' a good time."

—Johanna July

Seminole Negro Indian Scouts

During the late 1800s, even for a Black Seminole teenage girl, taming and herding horses was not common for females. But it was Johanna's role in the family. Her mother and sisters took care of the home and the cooking. Johanna July tamed wild horses for the United States army and local ranchers. Johanna spent her time outside; horses were her chore.

Her father, Elijah July, taught Johanna and her brother how to catch wild horses, hunt, and fish when they were young children living in northern Mexico. The family lived on a settlement established for the Black Seminoles, who were descendants of Seminole Indians and runaway slaves from Florida.

In 1871, her family moved to Fort Duncan, Texas, with many other families from their settlement. The Black Seminoles were given land in exchange for helping the army control the Apache and Comanche Indians. At Fort Duncan, Elijah was the *domador*, or the breaker of horses. After her father died and her brother left, Johanna became the *domadora*, or female breaker of horses, for Fort Duncan.

Besides taming the horses, July was also responsible for grazing the animals and collecting hay. She would take the horses out of

Johanna July Tidbits

♦ Johanna didn't like shoes. "I can sure get over de ground barefooted." Even when she was an old woman, Johanna preferred to walk barefoot.

♦ Johanna July, the horsetamer, would have been lost to history if it were not for Florence Angermiller. During the 1930s, Angermiller was hired by the United States government to collect oral histories of pioneer life. Johanna July was one of the people interviewed.

the corral and into the pastures. At the end of the day, Johanna would gather the horses and bring them home. While the horses fed in the meadow, Johanna collected hay. One day at the meadow "I got so sleepy, I said, 'Suppose I lay down an' take myself a nap' and den finish cuttin' my hay." But Johanna noticed the horses pointing their ears, snorting and pacing. She hollered for the lead horse, "Come Bill, come Bill." As Bill came running, all of the horses followed.

Johanna jumped up on a gray horse named Charley. From her perch on top of the horse, Johanna spied two Indian bandits galloping toward her at full speed. They were going to steal her herd. "I started runnin' an' run clear by de army post, me and all dem horses." Johanna ran the little gray horse as fast as it would go across the meadow to Fort Duncan. The full herd galloped behind her. She made it and the horse stealers gave up their pursuit. Even after her wild ride and the fear of bandits, Johanna said, "But that didn't break me. I was always out with dem horses."

Johanna's technique for breaking mustangs didn't always work as well as she

Also in 1871

* THE CHICAGO EVENING JOURNAL reports that a cow kicked over a kerosene lamp and started the Great Chicago Fire, which killed over 250 people.

* Cowboys drive 700,000 longhorn cattle along the 700-mile Chisholm Trail that runs from Texas to Kansas.

"I lived when I wanted to, the way I wanted to, and that is saying a lot for one mortal."

—Fannie Sperry Steele,
Three-Time Lady Bucking Horse Champion of the World

hoped. "Sometimes dey wasn't so wore out an' would take a runnin' spree wid me when dey got out in shallow water where dey could get der feet on de ground, and dey would run clear up into the corral," she said. But that didn't stop July from her broncobusting duties.

Johanna July broke many horses, but she didn't have as much luck with mules. Even though mules are a cross between a horse and a donkey, mules are known to be more stubborn and harder to break than horses. Johanna learned this well when "I helped my last husband break hosses an' mules." She had one mean mule and "he'd catch me by de clothes and toss me and shake me if he could get hold of me." Even though she tried and tried, Johanna said, "I never did break 'im, I got 'fraid of 'im." And Johanna was not the type to scare easily.

Johanna never rode astride on a saddle. An old scout at Fort Duncan, Adam Wilson, taught Johanna how to ride a proper ladies' sidesaddle. But she never really took to saddle riding, especially when she was young. Johanna July's preferred mount was bareback with "just a rope around der neck and looped over de nose." The TALENTED horse tamer never quit riding, although in her later years she chose to ride like a lady, sidesaddle.

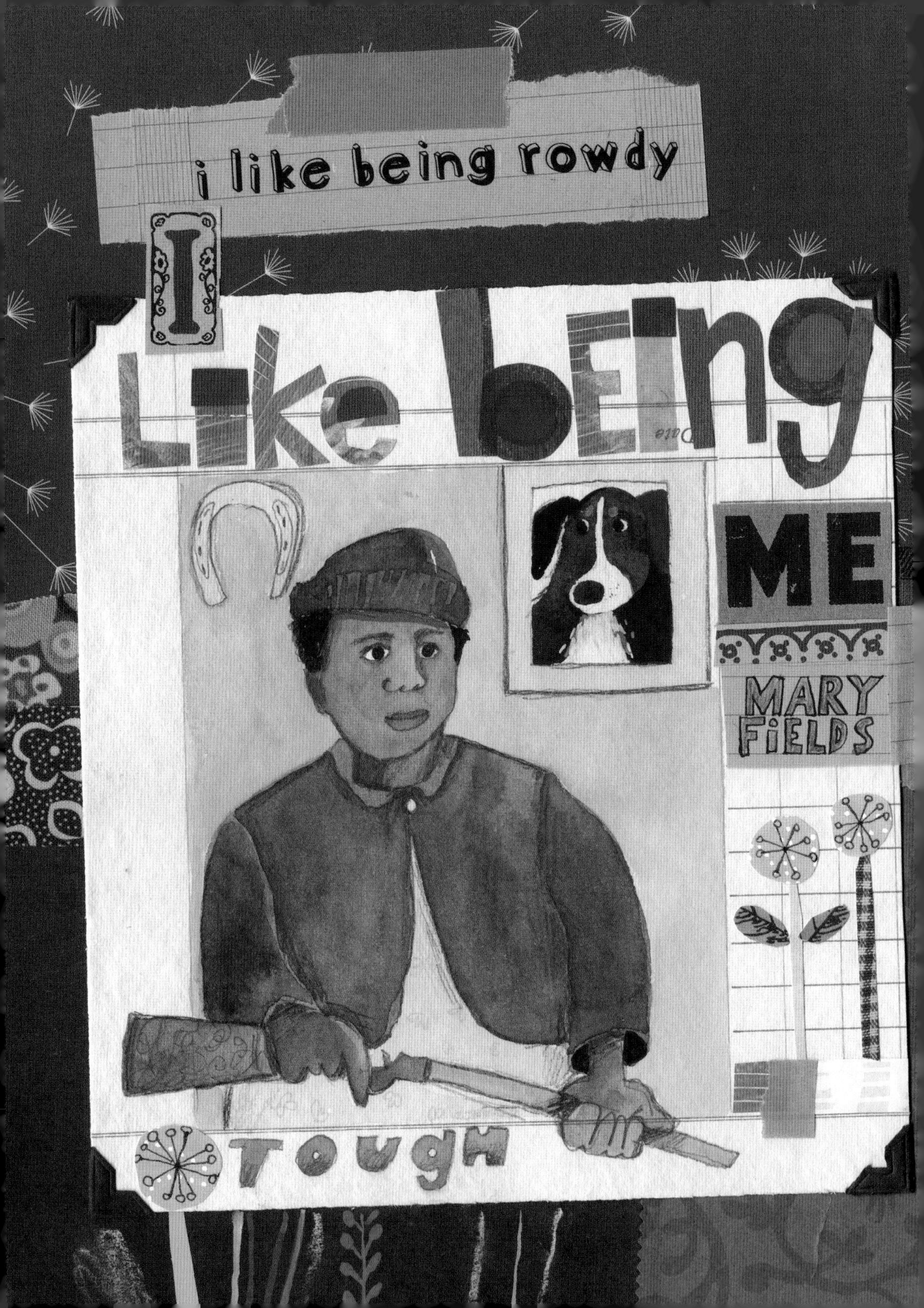
i like being rowdy
I like being
ME
MARY FIELDS
TOUGH

Mary Fields was big and strong. Mary was not a free black woman to be messed with. She was over six feet tall with two hundred pounds of muscle. Mary carried a pistol under her apron. She smoked handmade cigars, drank whiskey, and easily decked any man who wrongly crossed her path. She would also deck any man who acted unkindly to anyone Mary cared about.

Mary Fields in a horse-drawn wagon

Mary Fields Tidbit

Mary never knew her exact birthday, but each year, on a date Mary decided, the town celebrated her day. The school dismissed early, and Mary showered the children with treats.

From 1884 to 1894, St. Peter's Convent outside of Cascade, Montana was both her home and work. Mary oversaw much of the building at the Catholic mission and school. She took care of the four hundred chickens, did all of the laundry, and drove the freight wagon to retrieve supplies for the nuns.

Of course, Mother Amadeus didn't approve of the rougher side of Mary, but she had known Mary since she was a child. Mary Fields was a devoted worker and friend. And TOUGH. Tough is what got her through the harsh Montana winters and the necessary hard work.

After ten years of service to the nuns, Mary Fields was not going to let some hired hand disrespect her. Mary just figured the best thing to do with the mouthy upstart was to shoot him. Some accounts say she tried to shoot him while he

"A fearful woman never feels free."

—Judy Fort

← St. Peter's Mission School

cleaned the outhouse. Other accounts say she challenged him to a duel.

Everyone agrees shots were fired. Either she hit him in the backside and tore his

pants or the clean clothes hanging on the line got shot up. What matters is that

Mary Fields was expelled from the grounds of St. Peter's. The nuns really didn't

want to lose their helpful employee, but the Bishop felt Mary was not setting a

good example for the young girls attending the school. They were being taught to be proper ladies so they could fit into fine society. Shootouts were not within the training of a well-mannered Victorian female.

Once expelled from the convent, the nuns helped Mary set up a restaurant in town. Even though Mary's exterior was tough, her heart was soft. She just couldn't turn away a hungry person even if he didn't have the money to pay for the food. Her restaurant went broke.

But at the age of sixty-three, Mary Fields finally found her calling. She started delivering the United States mail in the mountainous countryside of Montana. Mary, the first African American woman to work for the US Postal Service, drove the mail stagecoach for eight years.

The nineteen-mile route was dangerous and rough. Mary smoked her cigars atop the stagecoach wearing men's pants, a heavy overcoat, and a skullcap. She still carried her pistol

Although Mary had a tough exterior, she had a soft heart and served food ⟶ at no charge to people in need.

and added a shotgun by her side. No bandit dared to rob Stagecoach Mary of her delivery. "Neither snow nor rain nor heat nor gloom of night" would stop Stagecoach Mary from making her mail rounds.

Also in 1884
* The first roller coaster opens at Coney Island, New York.
* THE ADVENTURES OF HUCKLEBERRY FINN by Mark Twain is published.

The devoted mail carrier never missed one delivery in eight years. If her wagon got stuck during severe weather, Mary would climb down, throw the mail sack over her shoulder, and walk to the settler outposts and remote mining camps. Her devotion made Mary Fields a well-loved local legend.

Huckleberry Finn book illustration by E. W. Kemble

After eight years of rugged postal service, Mary decided to slow down. In her early seventies, she opened a laundry in town. Mary grew flowers at her home, but she never grew soft. The mayor of Cascade gave Mary special permission to drink in the Cascade saloon. One day while sitting in the saloon, Mary jumped up from her chair and stormed out of the building. She walked up to a man on the street. The man had an unpaid two-dollar laundry bill with Mary and was trying to skip town. The saloon patrons watched as Mary punched him a good one and the man fell over. Back at her seat in the saloon Mary declared that the man's bill was now paid in full. Yep, Mary Fields was still TOUGH.

I am Mary Fields.

I am Mary Fields.
People call me "Black Mary."
People call me "Stagecoach Mary."
I live in Cascade, Tennessee.
I am six feet tall.
I weigh over two hundred pounds.
A woman of the 19th Century,
I do bold and exciting things.
I wear pants.
I smoke a big black cigar.
I drink whiskey.
I carry a pistol.
I love adventure.

I travel the country,
driving a stagecoach,
delivering the mail to distant towns.
Strong, I fight through rainstorms.
Tough, I fight through snowstorms.
I risk hurricanes and tornadoes.
I am independent.
No body tells me what to do.
No body tells me where to go.
When I'm not delivering mail,
I like to build buildings.
I like to smoke and drink
    in bars with the men.
I like to be rough.
I like to be rowdy.
I also like to be loving.
I like to be caring.
I like to babysit.
I like to plant flowers
    and tend my garden.
I like to give away corsages
    and bouquets.
I like being me, Mary Fields.

—Author unknown (some attribute to Mary Fields)

Sources

Asterisk(*) = suitable for younger readers.

GEORGIE CONNELL SICKING

Sicking, Georgie Connell. *Just Thinking.* Crosby, TX: Painted Word Studios, 2004.

*Weigand, Glorianne. *A Mare Among the Geldings: A Biography of Georgie Connell Sicking.* Adin, CA: 101 Ranch, 1998.

American Folk Website. Jack Lamb, "The Last of the Old-Time Cowboys: Interview with Georgie Sicking. Fallon, Nevada, August 22, 1992." http://www.americanfolk.com/bgq/features/feature2/.

Cowboypoetry.com Website, "Featured at the Bar-D Ranch, Honored Guest: Georgie Sicking." http://www.cowboypoetry.com/sicking.htm.

Range Magazine, "Confessions of Red Meat Survivors." http://www.rangemagazine.com/archives /fall2004/confessions.htm.

ANNIE OAKLEY

Russell, Don. *The Lives and Legends of Buffalo Bill.* Norman, OK: University of Oklahoma Press, 1979.

Kim-Brown, Caroline. "Little Sure Shot: The Saga of Annie Oakley." *Humanities.* May 1, 2006. Available from Highbeam Research, http://highbeam.com.

Ferguson, William A. "Following the Trail of the Legendary Annie Oakley." *Daily News* (Los Angeles, CA). January 26, 1997. Available from Highbeam Research, http://highbeam.com.

*Josephson, Judith P. "Annie Oakley: Sharpshooter from the Late 1800s." *Children's Digest.* June 1, 1996. Available from Highbeam Research, http://highbeam.com.

Gallop, Alan. "Queen Victoria Was Amused . . . and Bowled Over by Buffalo Bill Cody and His Famous Wild West Show . . ." *The Sunday Telegraph London.* January 14, 2001. Available from Highbeam Research, http://highbeam.com.

The Annie Oakley Foundation Website. Bess Edwards, "Annie Oakley's Life and Career." http://www.annieoakleyfoundation.org/bio.html.

"Tall Tales and the Truth." http://web.archive.org/web/20021015053658 /www.ormiston.com/annieoakley/tales.html.

Answers.com Website. "Biography: Annie Oakley." http://www.answers.com/annie%20oakley.

Dickinson State University Website. Tom Bushaw, "Annie Oakley 'Little Sure Shot.'" http://www2.dsu.nodak.edu/users/jbrudvig /Technology%20Projects/Internet%20Scrapbooks /Annie%20oakley.htm.

Lakewood Public Library Catalog Website. "Annie Oakley." http://www.lkwdpl.org/WIHOHIO/oakl-ann.htm.

Trapshooting Hall of Fame Website. Copy of "Powders I Have Used" by Annie Oakley. http://www.traphof.org/roadtoyesterday/march2001.htm.

CHARLEY PARKHURST

Metro Santa Cruz, March 5–12, 2003 issue. Daniel M. Hall, "The Strange Life and Times of Charley Parkhurst." http://www.metroactive.com/papers /cruz/03.05.03/charley-0310.html.

Mountain Network News Website. Joan Barriga, "Survival with Style: The Women of the Santa Cruz Mountains." http://www.mnn.net/cparkhur.htm.

The Museum of Art & History@the McPherson Center Website, Research Forum. Stanley D. Stevens, "Charley Parkhurst." http://researchforum.santacruzmah.org /viewtopic.php?t=62.

Shadows of the Past Website. Floyd D. P. Øydegaard, "She Was a Man!" http://www.sptddog.com/sotp/parkhurst.html.

SOURCES

TILLIE BALDWIN

ESPN.com Website. "The Calgary Stampede of Yesteryear." http://sports.espn.go.com/rodeo/news /story?id=3479721.

The Spell of the West Website. "Western Roots." http://www.jcs-group.com/oldwest/wildwest/western.htm.

TAD LUCAS

The Handbook of Texas Online. "Lucas, Barbara Barnes." http://www.tshaonline.org/handbook/online /articles/LL/fluhn.html

The TCU Magazine Website, Alum News. Rachel Stowe Master, "Riding Tall—and Sideways, Upside Down, Off the Back of a Horse." http://www.magazine.tcu.edu/articles /2002-03-AN.asp?issueid=200203.

LUCILLE MULHALL

Oklahoma Historical Society Website. "Oklahoma Journeys." http://www.okhistory.org/okjourneys/lucillemulhall.html.

The Spell of the West Website. "Lucille Mulhall." http://www.jcs-group.com/oldwest/wildwest /mulhalllucille.html.

Tulsa World Oklahoma Centennial Website. Gene Curtis, "Only in Oklahoma: Lucille Mulhall Was the First 'Cowgirl.'" http://www.tulsaworld.com/webextra/itemsofinterest /centennial/centennial_storypage.asp?ID=070724_1_A4 _Lucil24770.

CHARMAYNE JAMES

Anderson, Bruce. "Having a Barrel of Fun." *Sports Illustrated*. December 15, 1986. Available from SI Vault http://vault.sportsillustrated.cnn.com.

Valade, Jodie. "Barrel Racer Charmayne James Close to Ending Title Drought." *The Dallas Morning News*. October 28, 2002. Available from Highbeam Research, http://highbeam.com.

Fong, Tillie. "Rule Out the Barrel." *Rocky Mountain News*. January 23, 2004. Available from Highbeam Research, http://highbeam.com.

*Charmayne James's home page. http://www.charmaynejames.com.

LILLIAN RIGGS

Wegman-French, Lysa. "Chiricahua National Monument: Faraway Ranch Special History Study." 2006 National Park Service, Santa Fe, NM. U.S. Department of the Interior 129.116:72.

Arizona Women's Heritage Trail Website. "Lillian Riggs." http://www.womensheritagetrail.org/women /LillianRiggs.php.

CALAMITY JANE

*Calamity Jane. *Calamity Jane in Her Own Words*. Bedford, MA: Applewood Books, 1896.

Walker, Dale L. "Calamity Jane: The Woman and the Legend." *Montana: The Magazine of Western History*. October 1, 2006. Available from Highbeam Research, http://highbeam.com.

Blog Deadwood Website. "Calamity Jane, Texas Bill and Dirty Em Forever Leave Their Mark on Deadwood." http://deadwoodcalamityjane.blogspot.com/.

Cowboys and Indians Website. David Hofstede, "The Many Lives and Lies of Calamity Jane." http://www.cowboysindians.com/articles/archives /0601/reel.html.

Salon.com Website. Margot Mifflin, "The Real Calamity Jane." (Book Review of *Calamity Jane: The Woman and the Legend* by James D. McLaird.) http://dir.salon.com/story/books/review/2005/12/06 /mclaird/index.html.

SALLY SKULL

Sons of Dewitt Colony Texas Website. From *Legendary Ladies of Texas* (F. E. Abernathy, ed.), publication XLIII of the Texas Folklore Society. "The Story of Sally Skull." http://www.tamu.edu/ccbn/dewitt/skulllegend.htm.

Tough Women, Part 2.
http://www.caller2.com/autoconv/givensm99/givensm1.html.

TexasEscapes.com Website. Maggie Van Ostrand, "Sally Skull the Scariest Siren in Texas." http://www.texasescapes.com/MaggieVanOstrand/Sally-Skull-the-Scariest-Siren-in-Texas.htm.

JOHANNA JULY

Massey, Sara R. *Black Cowboys of Texas*. College Station, TX: Texas A&M University Press, 2005.

Angermiller, Florence. "Johanna July—Indian Woman Horsebreaker." Folklore Project, Life Histories, 1936–39. U.S. Work Projects Administration. Library of Congress. Available from http://ftp.rootsweb.com/pub/usgenweb/tx/kinney/bios/july.txt.

Blackpast.org Website. Sara R. Massey, "July, Johanna." http://www.blackpast.org/?q=aaw/july-johanna-1857-1946.

TexasEscapes.com Website. Linda Kirkpatrick, "Johanna Domodora of South Texas." http://www.texasescapes.com/LindaKirkpatrick/Johanna-Domodora-of-South-Texas.htm.

MARY FIELDS

Wagner, Tricia Martineau. *African American Women of the Old West*. Guilford, CT: Globe Pequot Press, 2007.

Graham, Art. "Mary Fields: The Story of Black Mary." *Montana: The Magazine of Western History*, Spring 2003.

Cascade Montana Community Website. Jennifer M. Drewry, "Mary Fields." http://cascademontana.com/mary.htm.

BlackCowboys.com Website. "Famous Cowboys . . ." http://www.blackcowboys.com/maryfields.htm.

The Life, Times and Adventures of Rambling Bob Blog. Rambling Bob, "Stagecoach Mary: Old West Legend." http://ramblingbob.wordpress.com/2008/06/19/stagecoach-mary-old-west-legend.

Western Americana: History of the American West Blog. Sue Schrems, "Montana's Stagecoach Mary."

http://westernamericana.blogspot.com/2006/04/montanas-stagecoach-mary.html.

GENERAL

Ash, Russell. *Fantastic Millennium Facts*. Willowdale, Ontario: Firefly Books, 1999.

Bernstein, Hoal H. *Wild Ride: The History and Lore of Rodeo*. Salt Lake City: Gibbs Smith Publisher, 2007.

*Furbee, Mary Rodd. *Outrageous Women of the American Frontier*. San Francisco: Jossey-Bass, 2005.

Grun, Bernard. *The Timetables of History*. New York: Simon and Schuster, 1963.

Jordan, Teresa. *Cowgirls: Women of the American West*. Lincoln: University of Nebraska Press, 1982.

Lackmann, Ronald W. *Women of the Western Frontier in Fact, Fiction and Film*. Jefferson, NC: McFarland & Company, 1997.

LeCompte, Mary Lou. *Cowgirls of the Rodeo*. Urbana, IL: University of Illinois Press, 1993.

Roach, Joyce Gibson. *The Cowgirls*. Denton, TX: University of North Texas Press, 1990.

Savage, Candace. *Cowgirls*. Berkeley: Ten Speed Press, 1996.

Trager, James. *The People's Chronology: A Year-by-Year Record of Human Events from Prehistory to the Present*. New York: Henry Holt and Company, 1992.

*Wills, Kathy Lynn and Virginia Artho. *Cowgirl Legends from the Cowgirl Hall of Fame*. Salt Lake City: Gibbs Smith Publisher, 1994.

*National Cowgirl Museum and Hall of Fame Website. http://www.cowgirl.net.

Suite 101.com Website. Vickie Britton, "Old West Female Outlaws: Renegade Women." http://www.suite101.com/lesson.cfm/19285/2829.

CREDITS

p. 35 top right: Detail of photographic postcard. Walter S. Bowman, photographer. #2004.265.2. Photographic Study Collection, Dickinson Research Center, National Cowboy & Western Heritage Museum, Oklahoma City, Oklahoma.

p. 35 bottom: Photo courtesy of Calgary Stampede Archives

p. 36: Titanic: © iStockphoto.com/Frank Boston

p. 37: Glenbow Archives NA-1029-21

TAD LUCAS

p. 39: Safety negative. Detail of photograph. Ralph R. Doubleday, photographer. #79.026.1634. Ralph R. Doubleday Rodeo Photographs, Dickinson Research Center, National Cowboy & Western Heritage Museum, Oklahoma City, Oklahoma.

p. 40: Ralph R. Doubleday, photographer. #Doubleday 153. DeVere Helfrich Rodeo Photographic Collection, Dickinson Research Center, National Cowboy & Western Heritage Museum, Oklahoma City, Oklahoma.

p. 42: Nitrate negative. Ralph R. Doubleday, photographer. #79.026.1938. Ralph R. Doubleday Rodeo Photographs, Dickinson Research Center, National Cowboy & Western Heritage Museum, Oklahoma City, Oklahoma.

LUCILLE MULHALL

p. 44: Library of Congress Prints and Photographs Division

p. 45: Oklahoma Historical Society Photo Collection, Courtesy of the Oklahoma Historical Society, 16588

p. 49: Murillo Studio, St. Louis, MO, Rose Strothman Collection, Courtesy of the Oklahoma Historical Society, 17778

CHARMAYNE JAMES

pp. 51, 52, 54: Women's Professional Rodeo Association

p. 57: © Kenneth Springer

LILLIAN RIGGS

pp. 59, 61, 63: National Park Service Intermountain Region Museum Services, Tucson, AZ

p. 60 left & right: Historic American Buildings Survey/The Library of Congress Prints and Photographs Division

CALAMITY JANE

pp. 64, 68: Everett Collection

pp. 65, 67, 70: Library of Congress Prints and Photographs Division

SALLY SKULL

p. 73: Palo Duro Canyon: © iStockphoto.com/Ronnie Wilson

p. 74: DeGolyer Library, Southern Methodist University, Dallas, Texas, Ag2008.0005

p. 76: Photo by Bob Thomas/Popperfoto/Getty Images

JOHANNA JULY

p. 79: Horse: © iStockphoto.com/WorldWideImages

p. 80: National Park Service, Fort Davis National Historic Site, Texas

MARY FIELDS

pp. 85, 87, 88, 90: Courtesy of Ursuline Archives, Great Falls, MT

p. 89: Library of Congress, Rare Book Reading Room